Certain
Silences

Clare Songbirds Publishing House Poetry Series
ISBN 978-1-957221-09-0
Clare Songbirds Publishing House
Certain Silences © 2023 Michael Sharp

cover design by Laura Williams French
cover photos courtesy of the US Library of Congress

Printed in the United States of America
FIRST EDITION

140 Cottage Street
Auburn, New York 13021
www.claresongbirdspub.com

Clare Songbirds
Publishing House

Certain Silences

Michael Sharp

For Ann Albuyeh, as always

And in memory

of my parents

Clare Carigiet and Stewart Sharp

Nous vivons à la merci de certain silences

Patrick Modiano

Contents

Prelude

The photographs in the album
were attached at random.
Some have slipped their hinge;
others are in unsealed envelopes.
Written in white ink,
the captions are as deceptive
as the past passed over.
The prints with serrated edges
were taken on a Leica IIIa
bought under the table
in a seedy Stockholm café.
The diaries and sketches
date from the summer of 1937.
Many of the drawings are witness
to jagged & unspeakable times.

Love Letters

Here's an irony . . .
a Wagnerian fancy-dress on deck.
Joséf is the German Chancellor.
You're in a dirndl skirt & bodice.
I'm Brünnhilda.

After you introduced me
to Lili in the Marienkirche,
I gave her the eye
as we knelt during Mass
that first day of September.

When the *Mongolia* left Danzig,
I ditched my Polish pilot
– later lost over Kiel –
and wrote love letters
I knew Lili couldn't answer.

Chance Encounter

It has started to snow.
The first storm of the year
drifting down the Vistula.
The Vienna Express is late.
Ours is a chance encounter.

The station waiting-room
is crowded and cold.
He looks like Olivier.
I am wearing mother's mink;
it is my Merle Oberon look.

He glances at me and smiles.
Our conversation is terse.
We whisper in English:
the *Grenzpolizie* will be wary
of the language he speaks.

The Great Zuninga

The synagogue in Sopot
has been burned to the ground.
I've slipped off my sandals.
The book I'm reading
was taken from the bonfire.

There's a trace of ash
under my fingernails.
One of the life-guards
has washed up on shore.
No one is laughing.

Even the Great Zuninga
& his Magic can't raise
a flutter from the crowd.
It's better, I think,
to go south this winter.

Nasty Man, Graham Greene

The woman opposite
is reading a copy
of yesterday's *Heute*.
I boarded the train
in Kraków.

You know Vienna?
Yes, from the pictures:
zither music, dark
streets, sewers,
an American named Holly.

He wrote Westerns.
I didn't like the story.
Nasty man, Graham Greene.
I remember the last frame:
the long walk home.

Oh, So Soho Soho

I took the tube to Blackfriars
and walked up Ludgate Hill
towards Eisenhower's office.

You stood outside St. Martin's.
I avoided your eyes
and entered the church.

A memorial service
was underway for victims
of a raid on the Isle of Dogs.

I found an empty pew.
You sat next to me.
I did not move aside.

As we knelt, I wanted you,
oh, so *Soho Soho*
in a Knightsbridge hotel.

Death By Water

I walked to his flat
on Farringdon Street.
The front door was ajar,
the bed unmade.
A frock lay on the floor.

A curtain flinched
on a jagged tooth of glass.
Someone had turned off the gas.
The cat shivered on the sill.
A cold wind blew.

In a Lyons' Corner House
somewhere on the Strand,
I imagined death by water,
the parachute in shreds
as he baled out over Kiel.

The Cable

It happened in Wales.
The airbase at St. Athan.
A cold December day.

The cable snapped.
The balloon broke free.

Death came quickly
to the boy manning
the mooring winch.

What was left of him
fell at your feet.

You cradled him
in your arms.
I closed his eyes.

It began to snow.
There was nothing to say.

Land Girls

As the war raged on,
I joined some land girls
in an allotment across the heath
and gazed in anger
as gun-dogs flushed

grouse from the bracken
and Hodge shouldered
his Purdey and fired
both barrels of 12-Gauge
into a blizzard of birds.

When he died, one of the women
I'd met during a YCL* rally
spat at your father's hearse
as it passed through Linn
on the way to the crematorium.

*Young Communist League

Portraits

Hodge gave mother
a tour of the house at Linn.
His book-lined study.
A Ruskin print above the desk.
An open *Tit-Bits* on his bed.

There were portraits
of the adopted child
in almost every room,
her eyes adrift like boats
and floating out of sight.

If you leave me alone
with that man again,
(she wrote in her diary),
I'll rip each one from its fucking frame
and throw them on a tip.

Unwanted

Something went wrong.
A botched tonsillectomy
that made your mother
flounce in affected grief
like a heaped marionette.

Cursing Hodge for owing
one of his cronies a favor,
she paid off whatever it was
and gave the unwanted girl
a home at Linn.

"You and your floozies,"
she hissed during the funeral,
"artists traipsing in & out,
those endless sittings.
No wonder the bastard's dead."

East of Snape

The cat stirred, circled me.
I was up before dawn.
A bloodless sun
rose east of Snape,
an icy wind blew.

I walked on the beach.
There were others about.
A woman in a hair-net
had half-draped the parachute
over the corpse.

Sand-eels slid in & out
of the drowned man's eyes.
"Thing's a long time at sea",
the woman said prodding him
with her stick.

Boys

It snowed that March.
The coldest day of the year.
You were late driving home.
The road from Cambridge
to Snape was slow going.

What a time I had of it.
There'll be no more after him.
The labor was endless,
the pain unbearable.
Push, the midwife said.

Mothering is for others.
How your sister had three,
two girls and *that* boy!
"I don't like boys," she'd say,
"they make your flesh creep".

Adrift in Darkness

The *Mongolia* left port.
I chose a cloche with a rolled brim.
You wore your college blazer.

We did not share a cabin.
It was late summer, 1937.

The weather was lovely.
The ship had a pool.
Your swimsuit looked like mine.

We docked in Danzig at noon.
The city was adrift in darkness.

There were three of them.
Thugs from a Bavarian *dorf.*
They shouldered you off the pavement.

"They'll die in Russia, you said,
"if Berlin has its way".

Stockholm

We went ashore in Stockholm.
There were eyes everywhere.
A man joined us in a café;
a quisling from Oslo.
He sold you a black market Leica.

You followed his advice
and photographed the old town.
I went into Bergström's.
"This is where Garbo sold hats",
the Norwegian said.

We gave him the slip,
found our way back to the docks.
I left my cabin door open.
Soon, riding along the cliffs
will be a thing of the past.

Charles Merryfield's Chrysler

You drove a blue Morgan.
How I loved that car.
We'd drive to Aldeburgh
and make love on the beach
under a North Sea sky.

We've something else now.
Charles Merryfield's Chrysler
out-swanks it by half.
They've a nice place next door.
I wish *we* had a pool.

Leave Hodge on the veranda
(I said under my breath).
It's cool inside the house.
The fig tree shades the window.
Let's fuck all afternoon.

Full Frontal

The envelope contains
a cache of photographs.
The address of a sanatorium
is written on the back
in bold gothic script.
I look at the prints.
One is of Andreas in profile.
In another, he poses
like Max Schmeling
sparring in a Berlin gym.
Both men are full frontal.
Her father is uncircumcised;
Toni has a modest penis.
Standing close, they are
like gods fused in marble.

Cousin Frieda

The chalet on the lake
has changed hands.
The climbers' hut
where they met in secret
has been razed.

The red Moto Guzzi
Toni bought in Bolzano
after he was cashiered
from the *Corpo Alpino*
rusts against a fence.

When the sanatorium
closed its doors,
your cousin Frieda took them in,
looked the other way,
let them be.

Distant Comfort

Alone in the Campagna,
they watch the mist
drift across Lago d'Averno,
hear the solitary cry
of a bittern in the reeds.

Above the unmade bed,
a Christ with torn hands,
reaches towards them
with outstretched arms,
offering distant comfort.

Three photos are missing;
only the captions remain:
Andreas und Frieda, 1946.
Der Nordwand (undated).
Death's Bivouac, '57.

The Cure

I look at them walking
in the garden at Cairn's View,
the old house overlooking
the ruins of a Roman fort
and the uneasy Tyne.

He is no longer aroused:
mother's lovely green eyes
now seem to him too large,
her cheekbones not high enough,
her red hair tumbling grey.

She wears her clothes
like a sea-widow swept
onto the rocks like kelp
and left to dry each summer
he left England for the cure.

A Web of White Spiders
(Berner Oberland,1957)

Traversing the Gods they are together
at last, belayed on the Wall between
Flat-Iron & Death's Bivouac, solo and
apart, the route severe. Two old lovers:
Andreas & Toni on a tight rope, facing
the Ogre, the scorch of ice, the snow
swirling like a web of white spiders .

The Kiev Road

As evening fell,
We walked back
over Clare Bridge
to the College
on Jesus Lane.
You played Messiaen's
Quartet for the End of Time
on the gramophone.
I remembered the women
under whose bodies
Lili had hidden
on the Kiev road
as enflamed men
kindled the night
with insolent fire.

Birdsong

Storm clouds drift
across the northern flows.
A cormorant flies its rock.
The sky is a smog of kites,
an abattoir at sunset.

Bog cotton drowns in peat.
A killdeer's skull
crackles underfoot,
sinks below my yellow waders
and nothing moves.

Heat-death is real.
Remember tomorrow,
Lili wrote from Prague,
The sound of birdsong
In a barn owl's egg.

Goya's Dog

When Teruel fell
to Franco's army
and the convent of Santa Clara
burned to the ground
and the dead sisters
were heaped like sacks
in the winter snow,
father wrote that *all*
his persuasions —
the power of prayer,
the patience of humility,
the hurt of suffering —
drowned like Goya's dog
in the cruel quicksand
of fascist Spain.

At a Loss

This photograph is dated 1939:
Clare College, Cambridge.
She's walked from Girton.
Deck chairs are on the lawn.
He's just back from Spain.

Lili has a new hairstyle.
A Slade School fringe
like Dora Carrington's.
Her skin is as fragrant
as orchids after rain.

They've waited a year for this,
the three together at last,
and all at a loss
as if (after Munich) *all*
had no codicil.

Remembering Radnóti

As he lived through
years of darkness,
so I live through his,
imagining the place
and the time, fearing
the breath of one,
the scream of another
for whom he dug
this ditch, finding
him in fragments
in a buried book,
a pocket of songs
that sing the terror
reasoned madness brings
its icy *ersatz* thrill.

Open Book

I took the bus to Vauxhall
and got off at The Cross.

Skirting the green,
no one looked up
as I passed The Black Dog.

Her touch was on the handle.
It would not turn for me.

I knocked on the side-door.
A curtain flapped like a shroud
in the window.

She was not at home.
An open book lay on the sill,

I read the underlined passage:
*"That is not what I meant at all.
That is not it, at all".*

The River Stairs

I walked along the Embankment.
It was a cold January day.
Barrage balloons fogged the sky.
Tower Bridge was crowded.
The Americans had arrived.

I stood on the river stairs,
watching the Thames
turn corpses into mud,
the girl I lost last night,
the woman I lost at dawn.

I did not think
I would find them here,
London blitzing into hell
as packs of Heinkels howled
across the Isle of Dogs.

Malice

Hodge sold the army
shoddy for uniforms,
made a fortune, lost it,
was taken to the cleaners
by one too many tarts.

When the firm collapsed,
and he left them nothing,
she threw out the portraits,
leaving his messy affairs
and the funeral up to me.

"Fuck him", she said
with pent-up malice,
as the cheap pine coffin
edged towards the flames
of the bleak crematorium.

Shabby Victorian

After the funeral,
ash settled on the graves
like flecks of Sahara dust.
In the long garden,
the winter trees
swayed like grievers
for those who might be next.
The day was wet and cold.
People from the village
with nowhere to go
invaded the house at Linn
and wandered around.
Not prime property,
someone said,
rather shabby Victorian.

The Candle

I left St. Magnus-Martyr
when air raid sirens
stifled the silence
of Wren's great church,
its dispassionate stone.

The Thames flowed in furrows
past the fish-market
as I walked through Southwark,
side-stepping a dead crow,
its eyes like rancid moons.

As the evening guttered
like the candle I'd lit for you,
the last of light flickered
through the blackened glass
but did not ease the dark.

The Banal Messiah

"I wonder what happened
to Hans Memling's *Last Judgment*
that Milwitz highlighted
in his painting of *The Interior
of St. Mary's in Gdańsk?*"

"Perhaps the Germans took it
when we weren't looking",
Lili answered with a wry smile
and took me by the arm
as we left the Marienkirche.

On the tram ride back,
a skinhead flashed us his tattoo
of the banal Messiah,
his undercut Austrian hair
and Chaplinesque looks.

Salt-Light

Undraped, the beloved and unkempt sea
gives up its nakedness to ones whose
nights are in light undimmed, who are
good in their nakedness, the beauty of
their skin luminescent, a bright darkness
of bodies, the unsaid breasts, the heave
and quiet fall of my beloved sleeping, the
tumult of stillness after arousal, a great
gale or fair riot against all wrong, a joy
in-folded, quarried within, our bed an
irrefragable tide of silence, the slate-jade
of eyes, our salt-light touch, its stir,
the quiet inviolable, our sound undraped.

The Bracelet
(Paris, 1951)

She sits alone
in a café on avenue Suffren -
L'heure de l'apéro -.
The bracelet on her arm
hides a lasting scar.

The hat she chose
is from Printemps.
It is slanted at an angle.
Her brown hair is cut
the way I liked it then.

The ring on her finger
we turned in secret.
It is hidden deep within.
She catches my eye
as I look her away.

93 Rue Lauriston

Despite the plaque,
people seem unaware
of what happened
in the dark salons
of 93 rue Lauriston.
When the register
was made public,
her name was not there,
and I wondered if you
simply imagined her.
Yet, *this* photograph
is of the girl you saved,
strapped to a chair,
her head shaved
and her frock ripped.

The Boy

Hodge rolled his own,
wore bespoke from Henry Poole,
shoes from Jermyn Street.
When Macmillan won in '57,
he joined the Labour Party.

The boy spent hours with him
on the veranda of the villa
on Buckingham Road
when *they* slipped indoors
for their Sunday nap.

His latest, a bookish widow
he'd charmed in Foyle's,
let the boy sit between them
as his hand meandered
up her skirt and moved around.

Spring

Clouds glide like herons
across the post-war sky.
I watch him from the window
cutting back the scorch,
dead-heading the roses.

It is Spring in Dover.
The winter trees are gone.
The frosts have passed.
Gorse blooms on the cliffs.
Silence is veined in leaf.

It is time to give birth.
I have hung up my crop,
moth-balled my jodhpurs,
stabled the grey mare
and thrown my life away.

The Third Landing

A diary entry recalls
leaving the boy under a clock
at five in the afternoon.
Someone had been assigned
to take him to the third landing.
An unlit passageway led
to a Piranesi-like staircase.
It circled upwards in a gyre
that ended at a forbidding door.
It was dark in the fetid room.
There was a view of the chapel
and the prison in the distance.
It was impossible to sleep.
The cries of the abandoned
kept him awake for years.

A Far Cry

They came after dark.
They forced him
to do what they asked.
When he would not,
they took him in turns.

He died in a bedsit
on Haverstock Hill,
a far cry from the manse,
its willows, terraced lawns,
sticklebacks in the beck.

Those who caused this hurt,
have all done very well:
trophy wives, fat accounts
with Hoare's, matching Jags,
boys at public school.

Swift Peace

Each honky-tonk he played,
the piano bars and clubs
(a Wurlitzer once in Hull)
all ended in a worn-out dive
in Camden Town.

The Sir Richard Steele
became his refuge.
His bedsit had no view.
He listened to the BBC,
his landlady's parakeet.

That winter, he slotted
coins into the meter,
closed the dingy curtains,
and let swift peace come
quietly dropping slow.

Messiaen's Birds

Music was an escape
after his mother's letters
were opened, their contents
read out loud and mocked
like Törless in Musil's book.

Before his death,
he saw Haitink conduct
Das Lied von der Erde,
took his girl to the ballet,
jazz at Ronnie Scott's.

As the gas fogged
that room in Belsize Park,
he closed his eyes
as Messiaen's birds
choked in the breathless air.

Saunders

When the boy was called
to practice, Saunders
rocked back & forth
like a metronome
in the dissonant room.

As he played, Saunders
kept the beat the boy couldn't keep,
his fingers tongue-tied
on the sallow keys,
all his scales at sea.

When the boy was excused
with a kindly word,
it meant much to him
those cold, desperately
lonely, winter days.

Vultures

A storm blew in.
He took the wheel.
There was hostility
& black ice all the way
from Cambridge to Snape.

Towards dawn,
the weather eased.
There were daffodils
on the banks of the River Deben.
The sun came out.

Arriving home,
they faced the birth
(*her diary records*)
like starved vultures
eyeing a mauled gazelle.

The Easing Hour

There is a hotel
in Sussex Gardens
that I know
that is discreet
and Greek.

I slip off
my loose-fitting
cotton frock
as the easing hour
is struck.

The shop-girl
is icy hot
like ghost-apples after frost
and slow to come:
our luxury.

Beckmann's Cabaret

I sat on the sea-wall
and watched the tide
roll in jade over blue,
the salt glistening
on her legs like frost.

We met in Hamburg
during the fire-storm
and drifted easily
into the bruised latitudes
of Beckmann's Cabaret.

I lied when my sister asked
if the fling was over:
"It happened in another city",
I said, "and besides,
the girl is dead."

The Serpentine

It's Autumn: the elms
on the Bayswater Road
are losing their leaves.
We swam in the Serpentine
that summer, after dark.

We climbed the railings.
He was wary, so I let my frock
fall slowly and looked away
as he stripped off
his civvies in a flash.

He left before dawn.
There were no goodbyes,
no last-minute tears.
When he disappeared over Kiel,
I erased men from my life.

The Undone Ones

You imagined them dying
in one of Zhukov's tank traps
between Minsk and Kursk,
or drowning on the Pripet
if they'd escaped the partisans
or like those lost today,
your MTB trawling the Channel
for corpses, the undone ones,
those airmen who won't return
to Graz or Unterbrunn.
You remembered Danzig,
the three thugs on Dluga Street
hard-shouldering you
into the gutter, their boots
an army on the move.

Killed-in-Action

I left his letters
unanswered, tore up
the postcards he wrote
from Warsaw and sent
to Lyon or Toulouse.

I ripped up the snaps
of the beach at Sopot,
the words he shaped into poems
like Apollinaire
in the Café de Flore.

When the telegram arrived
saying "killed-in-action",
I hid it between the pages
of the Proust Lili returned
to the library in Vichy.

A Pretty Bad Blitz

Where were you
when they bombed
Le Havre?

At the Savoy,
sharing "a pretty bad blitz"
with Coward & chums!

Where were you
when they bombed
Blankenberge?

At the Ritz,
tinkling the ivories,
tippling with bores!

Where were you
when this sketch
was made at Birkenau?

Sketchbook

I picked wildflowers
along the river,
arranged red campion
and yellow-flag
in a vase on the piano.

I entered the studio
and leafed through your sketchbooks.
I was startled
by a skill for drawing
I didn't know you had.

I gazed in horror
at a Belsen face
aging at the wire,
at things rotting
on wooden bunks.

One Last Fling

Leaving Eisenhower's HQ
on Grosvenor Square,
I walked to the National Gallery.
I sat down in front of Goya's
Doña Isabel Cobos de Porcel.

My eye caught hers
in a side-ways glance.
I glared at her and smiled.
You said *I* was more adorable
than all the ladies of Spain!

In the women's cloakroom,
I looked at my face.
I added a little rouge,
dabbed *Tabu* on my wrists.
One last fling, I murmured.

Cinq à Sept

Get out of town
before they come
and haul you off
to rue Lauriston
or somewhere worse.

If you don't leave,
our life will be over.
Go into hiding.
We'll meet in church;
you know where.

I'll put on a blue frock
and wait in a pew.
Have Colette cut your hair.
There is a *cinq à sept*
on rue Palatine.

Ash Wednesday

It was Ash Wednesday.
The day darkened
as I entered Saint-Sulpice,
a smudge charcoaled
on my forehead.

All are Welcome!
(the entry reads).
I sat next to you,
your hair was cut in a bob
like Louise Brooks.

We knelt together,
our hands touching
in affected prayer,
each of us sensing
others in the dark.

Tormentil

I left a trail of petals
for her to follow me
through the library,
across the college lawn,
and into the boathouse.

When she didn't come,
I pressed a spray
of loose-strife between
the pages of her sketchbook
open on the desk.

Later, I cut a sprig
of yellow tormentil
and left it wilting
in a half-empty bottle
of Médoc on the stairs.

Scorch
(For Mike Schuller)

Indigo, deep purple,
as white-mantled as a wave
of sea-green, Mary-blue,
all the irises in the garden
have faded overnight.

The burn has spread
from root to flower,
an unwanted tide
ebbing and flowing
from azure to rot.

The scorch we feared,
like an unseen plague,
has left things bare
as if an ocean had flamed
invisibly over the earth.

(Paris, 1941)

Fiery Ice

This photograph was taken
in a suite at the Bristol
on an October day.

I watch her from the bed.
She is as pale as the suicide
I once saw in a Vichy morgue.

I slip on a pair of Miss Rayne's,
trail *Soir de Paris* like a lit fuse,
my hair in a French twist.

Later, I hesitated
as she led me
into the ballroom,

her body smoldering
like fiery ice
in a red-hot Schiaparelli gown.

As if the Eagle

As if the eagle
had stolen the sun
for its lost eye,
the cruel burr of the sea
in the northern roads,
its brusque pidgin
of wave over rock,
the ragged heave
of kelp & sand eel,
the dead hoof
of war, its stamp
on a hundred days
of years, horse-gray,
feral, unfrocked,
corpse-cold.

The Frock

Slants of light cascade
through the shutters
of the safe-house in Vichy,
the Allier flowing by
like uneasy silk
on cold shoulders.
I am distracted.
Lili looks away.
I slip off the frock
– *snowdrops on blue cotton* –
I wore when word arrived
that a Polish pilot
had been downed by flak
during a night raid
over the Kaiser Wilhelm Kanal.

The Kiss

After the fire-storm,
I cycled across town
to the clinic where she
lay dying in a room
of drips & oxygen.

When I arrived
outside her window,
I whispered words
she could not hear,
might never feel.

The kiss I blew
touched her lips,
caressed her face,
circled her in its arms
as death settled in.

The Cobbles of Vichy

In a quiet corner
of the church of Saint-Blaise,
I began to scream
but the words
were not there.

Left all alone,
I could not speak
as if struck mute
by the mind's
distracting sounds.

I begged the cobbles
of Vichy to rise up
and stone those
who caused her death,
but they would not.

In the Mood

This was written
on a postcard of Sopot:
A field of yellow rape
stretched to the Channel.
A flight of gliders tugged
by four-engined Stirlings
and an army moving south.
Eisenhower stood by his car.
I was invisible to him
as he whistled a tune
that reminded me
of Wingy Manone
swinging "In the Mood"
Glenn Miller's way
before the Arnhem drop

Looking Back

I was at the wedding.
It was April 9th, 1942.
I'd walked across the park.
The sky was field-grey,
and a light rain fell.
He was in dress-uniform;
a Polish wing on his lapel.
I had met you before
at an embassy party.
We both wore backless gowns.
I begged you then
to run away with me.
Or was it you who asked?
Looking back, neither of us
can recall who spoke first.

Shitstupidity

Quelle connerie la guerre

Jacques Prévert

As we sat by the Cam,
someone poled by
in a punt and waved.
I said she was
the love of my life.

We spoke of Messiaen's
"The End of Time",
the shitstupidity of war,
all that fucking death,
the horror of Hiroshima.

We strolled arm in arm
over Clare Bridge
and talked into the night.
She left in the morning.
I never saw her again.

Pencester Gardens
(Dover, 1942)

A rogue Messerschmitt
strafed us as we ran
across the wet lawn
to the air-raid shelter
in Pencester Gardens.

You touched my cheek.
There was a small cut.
Shrapnel from a casing.
Blood spotted my blouse.
We had not met before.

You walked me home.
The house was in ruins.
I found my prayer book
smoldering in the rubble
like garbled fire.

The Hurt of Things

The mended bowl on our window sill
is flecked with gilt. It keeps its silence
like a chance hawk on a windy day.
It is a way of healing, of making better
the hurt of things by stitching sunlight
to a tilt of rain to ease each broken
piece and fragment into slants of gold.

After the Ceremony

All the bridesmaids
had perfect skin.
One died later in Ravensburg.
The best-man looked shifty,
the in-laws bored.

Her dress was white organza.
He wore his uniform.
Leaving the church,
she threw me her bouquet
over the arc of swords.

After the ceremony,
he returned to base.
I never saw him again.
She hid during the reprisals,
and I fled south to Vichy.

How Very Gatsby

He liked to show
me off in Selfridges,
have me twirl in front
of flash young things
at Muriel's, upstairs.
I wore zig-zag blouses
and long-flowing slacks.
At the Savoy he'd dazzle
the barflies to death,
drink them under the table.
"How very Gatsby",
I said as we tottered
back and said goodbye
outside his gin-soaked digs
on Farringdon Street.

A Studied Look

August in Paris.
There were geraniums in pots,
a slink of cats,
the whiff of hashish,
as I strolled through Passy.

Mine was a studied look:
hair in a French braid,
Balmain flats, Hermés scarf,
what looked like a Kelly bag
but wasn't, of course.

I drank a *pastis*
near Shakespeare & Co,
strolled through the flower-market
to a discrete house-boat
anchored along the quay.

A Prescription for Hurt

I went into a pharmacy.
There was something particular
that I needed for nerves.
The *pharmacienne* was from Sénégal.
Our eyes met.

I imagined her naked:
exquisite body,
short nails, tiny scars
on either cheek,
hair in a frizz.

Is there a prescription for hurt?
The *pharmacienne* smiled.
We became quick lovers,
sank briefly into cleanness,
cocaine, rented beds.

Hell's Girl

One orphic night
on a house-boat,
the Seine flashing by
like water-weed
through a net.

As I remember,
Rilke's *Sonnets*
lay open on the nightstand.
The *pharmacienne* was asleep
on rumpled sheets.

I heard her stir
as I slipped on my frock,
and, without turning,
tiptoed out like Eurydice
into *la grisaille*.

A Clash of Tides

Swallows flit in the elms.
Bats hang their cloaks
in the ruined hotel.
The fountain is clogged
with unlucky coins.

The tennis net sags
on the condemned court.
The garden where we met
when the all-clear sounded
has gone to seed.

As the haar drifts in,
the North Sea shudders
like a surfacing wreck,
its timbers breaking
in a clash of tides.

Tokarev

After a night together,
You hid the Tokarev
taken from a dead Russian
and kissed the girl goodnight
outside the cathedral.

You escaped the bombing
of Barcelona and returned
to the old neighborhood
in the Bari Gòtik
by the church of Sant Sever.

There was no trace of her.
You prized up a floor-board,
unwrapped the cloth,
held the gun to your temple
but could not fire the shot.

In the Distance

During the reprisals,
I planned her escape,
mapped out the journey
in a *Hôtel de passe*
on a street of red lights.

A circuitous route:
Vichy to the border.
Lili smiled uneasily
as I gave her papers,
keys to a battered Citroën.

She drove off unnoticed.
Nearing Ferney,
soldiers blocked the road.
In the distance,
Geneva sparkled.

A Ragged Circle

Dogs are unleashed
as they cross the river.
They attack on command
like starved terriers
at the Strasbourg fights.

Soldiers are entering
the deserted synagogue.
Soon the square will be
a ragged circle of old Jews
with violins and tin cans.

They're breaking into
the safe-house as I write.
One shoulders the door.
He flicks open a knife,
rips a blue frock to shreds.

The Afternoon Light

A faded snapshot
taken along the Arno.
I admire her skill
(you can read about it
in the *Corriere della Sera*).

She has set up an easel
overlooking a meadow.
Hers is a collective memory:
Katyn's leafy trees,
the ravine at Babi Yar.

As the afternoon light
glances off the river
like white impatiens,
I lean forward and kiss
the numbers on her arm.

Japanese Maple

We've planted
a Japanese maple
in a quiet corner
of the long garden.
It has five or four leaves.
When it grows
it will give us shade,
a place to be.
There'll be no words —
no *Here Lies* or *Ci-Git,*
no *Called Back* —
and if they cut the tree,
a bench will sprout
and with it, perhaps,
a tiny plaque.

Storm of Light

I lit a candle for you in the forlorn hope
your beautiful face might return my gaze
in this echoing church by a darkening river
the hour appropriate, your eyes flashing
a storm of light, as if, here, like Rilke
in his deeply imagined life, a denied presence
of the unseen might somehow be revealed.

Dover Beach

I stood at the window.
You came to my side
in the early hours,
easing night from day,
bringing warmth.

You stayed with me
when others left,
when the streets darkened
and some we knew
were herded east.

We made a life
on Dover beach,
the sea on fire at sunset;
gulls and guillemots
the only ones to call.

A Chance Hawk

The apartment has been sold.
There are plastic flowers
in the window boxes now.

The chandeliers have gone.
The curtains taken down.
The cloisonné auctioned off.

Before they came, I sat
at the window one last time
and watched the birds:

blue-tits, sparrows, robins,
a magpie in the limes,
seagulls adrift on land,

a chance hawk
brooding like a leaf
in the oracular sky

Coda

I have cleared the desk
where she sat in the dark
watching the lights of the barges on the river.
Before the concierge arrived,
I removed the last page of her diary:
"June 2nd 1983, my beloved left today".
I hid the album, diaries, and sketches
in a metal box
in the mezzanine room
until there is time
for others
to reimagine its contents.

Acknowledgements

"Salt-Light" (*Long Poem Magazine,* London)
"The Hurt of Things" (*Erbacce*, Liverpool)
"Scorch" (*Honest Ulsterman*, Belfast)
"As if the Eagle" (*Causeway/Cabhsair*, Aberdeen)

Michael Sharp was born in England and graduated from the Royal Conservatoire of Scotland and holds graduate degrees from universities in England and the United States. His doctorate is from the University of Wisconsin -Madison. He teaches English Literature and Caribbean Studies at the University of Puerto Rico in San Juan. Michael Sharp's poetry has been published on both sides of the Atlantic. *Certain Silences* is his second book for Clare Songbirds Publishing House.

www.ingramcontent.com/pod-product-compliance
Lightning Source LLC
Chambersburg PA
CBHW031448120626
46545CB00006B/2608